MW01014411

Once Removed

Also by Elizabeth Bradfield

Approaching Ice

Interpretive Work

Once Removed
Elizabeth Bradfield

POEMS

A Karen & Michael Braziller Book

PERSEA BOOKS   NEW YORK

Copyright © 2015 by Elizabeth Bradfield

All rights reserved. No part of this book may be reproduced or transmitted in any form or by any means, electronic or mechanical, including photocopy, recording, or any information storage and retrieval system, without prior permission in writing from the publisher. Request for permission to reprint or make copies, and for any other information, should be addressed to the publisher:

Persea Books, Inc.
277 Broadway
New York, NY 10007

Library of Congress Cataloging-in-Publication Data:
Bradfield, Elizabeth.
[Poems. Selections.]
Once removed : poems / Elizabeth Bradfield.—First edition.
        pages ; cm
Includes bibliographical references and index.
ISBN 978-0-89255-463-8 (original trade pbk. : alk. paper)
I. Title.
PS3602.R3396A6 2015
811'.6—dc23
                    2015002089

First edition
Printed in the United States of America
Designed by Rita Lascaro

for Phyllis, Betty Rue, and Gracie
teachers all, beloved and missed

CONTENTS

I. Distance Education

II. Interlude, Adrift

III. GETTING OUT

Once Removed

I.
Distance Education

Accuracy is always the gateway to mystery.
—DENISE LEVERTOV

We All Want to See a Mammal

We all want to see a mammal.
Squirrels & snowshoe hares don't count.
Voles don't count. Something, preferably,
that could do us harm. There's a long list:
bear, moose, wolf, wolverine. Even porcupine
would do. The quills. The yellowed
teeth & long claws.

        Beautiful here: Peaks, avens,
meltwater running its braided course. But we want
to see a mammal. Our day our lives incomplete
without a mammal. The gaze of something
unafraid, that we're afraid of, meeting ours
before it runs off.

        Linneaus was called
indecent when he named them. Plenty
of other commonalities (hair, live young,
a proclivity to plot). But no. Mammal.
Maman. Breasted & nippled
& warm, warm, warm.

Why is this? [handwritten annotation]

THE TRURO BEAR

I am lonely for the bear
two towns south and heading
here. The bear, too, is lonely.
For what other reason would it
swim the canal then walk
the whole of the Cape toward us?

Mornings, we rise early, drive, look
in places we'd like to see it. Evenings,
the same. Scat, a track, a tuft of hair
would be enough. We don't mind
ticks or briars although we're troubled

when highway drivers spot it and not us.
One man catches it on infrared
in his back yard: lightbulb of a hind end,
narrow legs sauntering. Orleans, Wellfleet,
Depot Road, then at Bradford and Conwell,
the busiest corner in town. This

will be the summer I don't return
to Alaska. This will be the summer
I won't visit the woods where I learned
to walk with bears. One afternoon

in the height of it, steaming home
from a day on the water (no bear
at Race Point, no bear at High Head), we pick up
a distress call from a boat off Wood End Point:

the *Black Bear* has lost power, is being set
ashore. We turn west, stare. The *Black Bear*.
I'm not kidding. Rust stains every plank
of its dark hull. We watch the crew dig out
an anchor, drop it. We stand by
until they feel it catch. Bob says
they made the same call yesterday.

The next day or the one after, officials dispatch
teams with darts and nets and the bear
is gone. Things are fine for a while,
although our market chitchat feels
small and mean. Then we hear

it's headed our way. We hear
it's climbed a Boston suburb's tree where
they shot it and trucked it west again
to the woods they think it came from. But

it was coming back. It had found plenty here:
berries, acorns, skate tails on the beach,
ground unclaimed. I was lonely at that
age. I wandered, restless. Now

I will be, the woods will be,
the ponds and bogs and briars will be so
lonely for the bear. We know how alive we were

at its low shrug. For a while, at least,
we were reenchanted, our gossip urgent
and hopeful. We loved our loneliness then.

Ritual

Each morning, the truck comes early
to the ocean lot. The man has

an out-of-fashion moustache. The dog
is a golden lab. Overweight, eager.
The truck is red and newly-washed

always. He lets the dog out, rolls down a window.
Sit, he says. The dog, tongue out, does.
Not reluctantly, about to bolt, but like a suckup.

Slowly now, the truck rolls. *Come.* And the dog
follows around the lot, heels the driver-side wheel
through thin-drifted sand. The dog does not

divert to the beach, does not take off
into rabbit-hunkered brush.
Like a circus pony, it trots. What

the dog thinks of the man, the man
of the truck, the truck of the slow circling
dog at its side, the dog of that bright red

ringleader—what I should think of any of it
as terns plunge for fish and the ocean
continues gnawing the shore and I decide

to not walk the soft sand but sit in my car
and watch it all, window cracked—tell me. Tell me.

RIGHT WHALE: DEATH AS SPECTACLE

The bulk ashore not yet fetid, but surely
close. Tire tracks deep in sand where tractors
tried to haul it up, chain around the tail stock.

There was a steady stream of visitors, for who
wouldn't want to see or didn't feel obliged
to stand near and take measure of

a right whale on the beach? Still, I don't know
that it was anything good in me, anything kind
or gentle that made me think my grandmother,

visiting, would want to be there. We trudged
into a hard wind toward the yellow flags
staked around books of flensed blubber.

Biologists clambered the ribs and bonnet,
measuring, cutting in, digging for cause.
I was young. Bulk and death fascinated me, but

my grandmother had already put behind her tonnages
of grief. The colors of the flesh—black skin, white fat,
red meat—were steeped in late fall light. Baleen listed

from its jaw, nodding to wind, waves, footsteps over the body.
How beautiful, I thought. How lucky. How sad.
This was spectacle and, too, a reprobation of spectacle.

Her face was composed in the soft blank of looking.
Really, I have no idea what she thought.

IN THE INNER HARBOR

You can see the *Chico Jess* sunk
dockside. Pilot house and deck glow
through harbor water, shift
with light, tide, and the seasons
of plankton. Mast and radar flag up
through chop, through sheen.
Some say scuttled. But maybe
just the natural fate of an old boat
that's worked itself to rust and rot
by working the waters through their fish.
Down now to what once was trash:
skates and dogs. Either way,
it's tied to the pier where it sank,
ringed by orange containment booms,
still moored between the *Carol Ann*
and *Jersey Princess*.

      Off the wharf's end, gannets feed.

      They soar with one eye tipped then
          stall   fold   javelin
      and pull air down with them, trajectory
      visible and true as guy wires.

      Small fish caught and swallowed before
            wings half-open

                              a gleam

                  in the bluegreen,
          they rise
      shake the water from themselves
                        take flight.

The *Chico Jess* doesn't rise,
though we want it to, this relic
of a time when we raised boats
not because of seepage but
for salvage. The town debates
who should foot the bill of its removal.
The gannets, hunting among the moorings
and pilings of the inner harbor, work
through water we once feared
would erase us and now hope,
despite all facts, might manage it.

November, Sunk

The story is simple. *Twin Lights* was dredging
for scallops off the point, got caught up
on some gear, and when the skipper turned to get her free
a wave came wrong. She rolled right over.

The flipped hull bellied like a bloated whale. *Glutton,*
tending a line of pots nearby, saw it
happen, got there quick enough
to fish out the mate. Someone put on

gear, swam over, knocked and knocked
and tried to hear some rap come back
other than chop. The *Twin Lights* went down
slow, then fast. Sunk.

Papers and spilled coffee and haul and gear and captain
and all. Another ghost. Another service

for one *lost at sea.* In the church's high glass,
winter light seeps through waves, prows,
men bent to nets. The current
off the point is strong. Divers

and machines will search for remains, stuff
will wash up on the outer beaches and next spring,
when we pass over the spot as we will each day
of the season, we'll snag on memory. In the pilot house,

we'll splice versions and details, making
an eye of the bitter end, securing ourselves
against drift, against time's blur, and so
to our place in this water.

Historic Numbers of Right Whales
Skim Feeding off Cape Cod

Who would expect their appetite
would come to seem ominous?
But now I know

they are voids of hunger. They plough
a field of plankton, turn,
plough again. They strip the water

like loggers on a clearcut.
The bay this spring seemed overrun
by stern, enormous beetles:

black, vaguely military, inexorable.

Poor plankton, adrift
in flailing clouds, poor blushing copepods
with delicate antennae, watermelon scent—

you don't stand a chance.
Week after week, right whales
eat the bay down

until they have to leave it.
Time and proximity have made them
monsters. This must be how it was before.

Misapprehensions of Nature

That bees are improper
        because they have a queen
no king. That crows plant

acorns, twist them into soil,
        properly spaced, to serve
as future roosts and manta rays

wrap divers in the dark
        blankets (*mantilla*)
of their wings.

That dolphins
        love us, that deer love us,
and the kit brought in and given milk

is just as happy. That we can know
        what it is for a fox
to be happy.

        **

Two men bought a lion
        at Harrods, reared it
in their small apartment,

released it (reluctantly) to savannah.
        And then, years later,
sure that it would know them,

went and called its pet name
        into the grasses.
It ran toward them.

That they would be mauled.
        That perhaps they should
be mauled. But it

tumbled them, licked their faces:
        Everyone was crying.
        We were crying,
even the lion was nearly crying.

On the Habits of Swallows

A month since I swam out to the middle of the pond toward a flock
of swallows, trying to convince the sky I was a turtle, a log, a bit of
nothing. Hoping murk would hide the pale articulations of my legs.
A month since I knew I had to try and write it. *What were you waiting for?*
It happened more than once. *More than once?* The second time
I swam out hard, teeth clamped, because someone—a woman
with three kids—had found the path and five-foot beach
I'd come to consider mine. The girls were loud and presumed
their splashes cute. *And were they?* From the middle of the pond,
distant, I guess they were. Some manifestation of human joy, messy
and concerned with its own bright surfaces. *Okay. Sure.*
But is that it?—No.

        But I want to suspend for a bit, hover
like I did treading, oaks ovaling the sky, road-sound almost
ignorable because the rest of it was so still, so idyllic, so self-in-a-painting.
Get on with it. I almost can't. To put it down lets you evaluate,
opine, judge. *Get over yourself.* Okay. I was trying to be nothing
to startle from because in the low light of not-quite-sunset
close to a hundred tree swallows rose, gathered,
then came low to hit the water,

                hit the water, like skipped stones
that could lift and shake themselves and rise to circle again. They were going
for water-striders, which covered the surface like spilled pepper. They were
bits of the day given appetite. Around my head, at eye level,
their fist-sized bodies hit the pond then rose through the strange machinery
of their voices. Was it Aristotle who thought they wintered buried
in the pond, somehow breathing there? *Aristotle, yes.* Well,
summer coming to an end, it almost seemed like they were
making forays toward that. *Linnaeus thought it too, you know.*

Even him. The point is, I was in the water
and they, beaks audibly snapping, blue neck-feathers glinting—*not
really blue, of course*—they hit and hit the surface
around my head, and at last—listen—at last I
was the surface, too. Or as close to that as I could ever get.

The Problem of Syllogism

I've seen tandem fins rise through dawn water,
black surfaces toward each other, white to horizon.
It takes some time to remember the kite body
between, the frowned mouth beneath,
the whip tail's taper. I've never thought

an airplane, even one abstracted to glint in blushed light
or a holiday squadron executing flips and turns, beautiful.
Home, fighter jets scrape the air above my walk. Sometimes
high enough to blur with mosquito-whine. Sometimes
low, screaming fierce joy at the stick. The rays

in clear water look like a pilot's dream of an airplane,
fluid and alien. Sometimes they launch themselves
toward sky, glint and flop. And sometimes they swim
in squadrons, as if scales of some vast other form. Then, resisting,
I resent what I'm forced to concede. I thrill a bit to the gut.

August Song

hush the oak, leaves stiff with coming fall

hush the flood tide into dry marsh

a yellowlegs hushes down on stiff wings

      hush mind   hush mind

hush of water at its bright knee-knobs

there's a hush to the sky: grace of distance

and time will hush what hurt

what greater hush is there than a boat aground

then   lifted by tide?

grass hush midge hush wind-pushed

hush the days into sleep's relief

stillness   at the core

your frenzy stills nothing

OBLIGATIONS TO THE UNPRECEDENTED

I can't hold both facts
in my mind at once: that
there are so few and that there are

so many. Two thirds of the world's
North Atlantic right whales
can be seen from the parking lot

which was a drifted mess of snow
and sand a month ago and in a month
will be too crowded to bear. Early spring

usually it's just locals parked
to read the paper or feed gulls. Today
it's packed. Plates from Connecticut, Quebec.

Some of us who live here, though,
haven't come to look—are
scrambling to open shops

for the odd boom or muttering
it's all another scheme
to boost the shoulder season.

But given how well we've normalized lack,
when historic plenty slaps its fat palm down,
shouldn't we show up?

A Further Explication of Irony

Penikese Island, 1973

Another night on this island you could steal away from, given ice
or jet pack. Mainland clear in good weather but too far
by crawl or backstroke. You're a boy. Thirteen. Fifteen.

You've done something to be sent here. Petty
theft, knife fights, worse. Nights, you can't help it,
you think of the lepers, scabby and shuffling, here

before it was a school. You can almost
hear them. No traffic. No fathers. No dogs
rattling chain link as you walk their alleys. But still,

sounds. Wind, mostly. Waves. The scrabble of mice. Then,
mid-summer, a new noise half mutter, half scuffle.
And I bet you could give a shit about ecology,

demography, or much of anything beyond getting out or
getting up the pecking order so that nights,
at least, you could sleep instead of listen. Did you

know there are birds that spend their lives at sea?
Once a year they're forced in to nest, so find the smallest,
most isolated shore, make secret flights to and from

a burrow at the edges of light, exchange odd conversations
in darkness. At sea their wings nearly slice the wave caps.
You've never seen such clear delight in soaring.

This is what I envy: you were there. You
slept lightly and heard a rustle gone at daybreak.
Your old stone walls were thick enough to be fissured

and yet still sound. Why did you tell?
And why did that teacher listen to you and then
listen with you at night? How did he know

to recognize a sound he'd never heard? You found
Manx shearwaters nesting in Massachusetts.
None of the books knew about this yet. Those birds

were truants, using what's almost abandoned.
For them, your exile was refuge.

Distance Education

In Unalakleet and Gambell, my students,
teachers' aides who need this class
to keep their jobs, learn this week that they must care

about the semicolon. More
than their properly punctuated sentences,
I want to read what stories
they tell themselves to make it matter.

I don't know when murre eggs
are ready for harvest or when
walrus meat tastes best.

Hard to care about the split
infinitive when ice storms,
when past dues, when shore erosion.

I assign homework they don't do
because they had to take kids
away from fathers or because

cloudberries ripened in the bog.
I look at my spreadsheet of work done
and points assigned. The icon for its program
is green as new shoots of pushki. I fail them.

VALKYRIE

Race Point, April

First whale watch of a calm day. We're quiet
with coffee, scanning for blows in the rip,
then *holy shit*. On the point, hard up
near the lighthouse, a scallop boat.

People gawk under the bow,
dwarfed and shadowed. It is
upright. Perfect. Aground.

We bet they made their last run then set
the autopilot on a straight course for the harbor,
blasted tunes, sorted catch, zoned out,
ran hard and hit the point dead on, dock

straight ahead but sea interrupted
by sand. There's a truck on the beach. Then
a backhoe. High tide will come soon enough.

Back at the pier, we tell the stories
told by those who aren't the subject
this time: drugs, sloppy crew. Someone
calls the skipper a dumbfuck

and we all nod. Maybe it'll float off fine. Maybe
we won't have to drum up sympathy or take it
as a caution. It'd be nice to keep it

a good yarn, shake our heads, laugh
at their luck and ours being first of the fleet
to see it. They could have chucked a rock
and hit the tower meant to warn against just this.

An Apology of Sorts

Dear hiker, I was the one who ripped your amateur flagging
from the trailside oak and sweetfern, mouth set

> like my mother's as she picked up dirty socks
> from the corners of the house—exasperated,
> determined, aware she fought the inevitable.

It was also me who kicked apart
your stick arrow and erased your dirt-X.

> One day she declared that anything
> on the floor come morning would go
> straight to the curb.

At the fork near the overlook, ocean smell nearly certain,
my pockets were full. I wadded and gripped your markers.

> Out of childhood's deep sleep, I stumbled
> toward breakfast. My backpack, my right slipper
> gone. It was as if the house itself had risen against me.

Messy, lazy, careless. Oh, I did think of you, whoever you are,
fumbling home, anxious about direction and time. But

LNT

> I was full of firm tenderness and certainty
> that the woods unmarked by your passage
> and even your short-lived confusion and my
> part in it were, after all, for the best.

Cultural Exchange

Ucayali River, Peru

Sad →7 happy

The passengers, as instructed, bring useful gifts
—pencils, hairbands, soccer balls—instead of candy

or money. I collect them, sweep them
into garbage bags to lock in the ship's hold

for later distribution in the villages.
Pedro wants to know if he can take

a bottle of gummy vitamins
home to his kids. I've got my eye

on some little notebooks. I suppose
we both refrain. But everyone wants

the tennis-racket-shaped bug zapper. So, after
some discussion about ethics, Juan keeps it

behind the bar. The captain stops by and swings
after he manages a tricky bend. The woman

from Cabin 12 who's been sick all trip and now
is up and about, giddy, swings.

Diego and I watch, slap our ankles. At night,
the ship nudges into the bank and someone ties

the bow to a tree. The guards prop their rifles
by the hammocks on the stern. Fishing bats hit

the low-lit water. Someone has music on low.
Someone murmurs to home on his cell

and someone takes the racket out
and dances with what dances in tropical air,

swings through the swarm that swarms the dim deck lights,
accompanies himself with zap & flash.

In the morning someone sweeps the decks
of what is not confetti and yet is evidence

of some victory, some celebration we now share.

Deer Hunter

The boat rides over a swell. I'm trying
to not stop looking out toward what seems flat, familiar
but could—roseate terns to starboard,
underwings oranged by sunset—
rise, unbidden, as we return
from the whales, which we do
three times daily through September.

Jack closes the navigational chart
on the computer and opens
his favorite game: *Deer Hunter.*
Woods. Hills. Snow
not unlike static. A deceptive
pheasant. He scans

the digital trees for digital
movement, the rising of branches
that are not branches.
                        To port: again
the expanding evening, the picturesque
lighthouses (again), the dunes (again).

Look: Over that rise
on the screen. Is that a buck
stepping into range, chuffing breath?
Should he mouse the gun
to do its work?
                        I should go out on deck
to reflect what wonders we have met,
explain again the mechanics of baleen.

Jack lifts the real binoculars from their place
around the binnacle. The screen blinks

dark. The buck
wasn't there after all, and
without Jack, nothing in the woods
is moving.
                        Ahead, it seems
there may be something in the water.

II.
Interlude, Adrift

Travel of the Light

In the old north, maps were not made
from paper, but carved from rare drift
then carried in a mitt, followed by touch
in that dark until peaks spoke
to peaks. Aligned as *home.*

> Let me search back, let me search
> for landmarks, for clear
> and fixed positions.
>   I remember
> the airport in Tucson. You
> found me at my gate, waiting
> to leave. *Love*, you said, and marked me.
> That waypoint.   That beginning.

South Pacific maps were baskets
of wind and wave, vector and junction.
Sky breath   pitch and yaw   enough
to cross what seems   featureless.

> Some pasts we need
> to be untraceable.
>   When she left
> her house, my grandmother
> threw out sixty—seventy?—years
> of diaries. She did not offer them.

I've always loved the skillful monsters
and unsettled edges of parchment maps.
I can tell how hard they were trying.

> My heart, my heart—I am so often lost.
> How do we map our time apart?

When the first to southern ice wandered it, were
blinded by its days-long glare, they ate birds,
found rocks inside the gut. Evidence of shore
beneath the shore that continues to revise itself.

How and when do we fix memory or learn
what to forget? A navigator knows
time and distance magnify
small errors.
                    What
is the course steered
compared to the track made good?
What set?   What drift?

In laboratory dark, birds leap toward
their routes. Their inked feet
prove again and again that they know
which way (and when) to begin.

Deliquesce: A Meditation in Seven Parts

I. Verb: *To melt away or disappear as if by melting*

definition
format

How many hours have I stood before water
attempting this? And when did the urge begin?

I can feel concrete beneath my feet, wooden rail under hand,
wind, blackberries scenting up the steep, clay bank

that the stairs followed down in a suspended, wobbled reach
to the beach. Always

a gull hovering at eye level, at rest in wind. Was I five?
Five, nine, sixteen, I stood and stared at the bay,

at water, at what I might (oh, soft persistent hope) dissolve to.

Italian has a better word: *liquescere*. To

become liquid.

> *Liquescere.   liquescere.*

the world whispered, whispers to me.

II. Chemistry: *Become liquid by absorbing moisture from the air*

Dawn on the bow. Or some hour early enough to be,
for at least a while, alone. Firm horizon denied by mist. Prow

rocking forward into swell (forward, only forward,
it always seems). The air's liquid palpable

in silence. Horizon of skin blurred. The body's liquid not
separate. Pulsing, held, selfless.

We are, by vast percentage, sea.

The eye can stand to be open only through tears. We see
wetly. Salt wet sea. A bit of spray and I taste it. Ocean.

There is no voice, no other to ask or exclaim and so disrupt
this delicate experiment that, to survive, I run.

Sky becomes water, water, sky. And I . . .

dissolve   dwindle
disband   disperse   dissipate
become delinquent to the self

III. *Liquidare,* Italian. *To liquidate; to get rid of*

Yes, says the fog edge. *Yes* the spindrift,
the mare's tail, the nimbus, the veil cloud's velum
upon which nothing can be written.

Yes, ice slurries from a glacier.
Yes, ice brash and rafted, driven by wind.
Willing to dissolve, despite the fact that it

could not resist.

IV. Origin: *From the Latin "dissolve," mid-18th century*

Enlightenment, what you've given us.
The unweighting of ideas and architecture,
science itself freed to reach beyond
earth's edge, peer beneath the ocean's lens:

Halley's diving bell lowered, a man
as its clapper (church of sea),
breathing not with but at least beside
fish, squid, barnacle, scallop.

And the sky, too, breached. Stars
seen not as a dome's flaws
but tidal, drifting heat.
I never wanted to become the night sky,

to disappear into that height. The heavens
are a poor attempt at sea.
They whisper nothing, just burn
in silence. At night the sea

has much to say to itself, to us.
It has its own stars. To be within
them, body a shadow in phosphor,
is at once closer and further from my goal

than anything. I am nearly . . . I am not.

    deliquesce, hisses a wave to the sand
    deliquesce, deliquesce, deliquesce
       Yes

V. Biology: *To branch into many fine divisions, as bronchioles*

Tide flows in, floods all narrowings, all ends and origins.

       What can float is lifted. What can't be lifted

           is covered. Surface glint hides

               resistance in sky.

VI. Botany: *To become fluid or soft on maturing, as some fungi*

Do we become softer with age, or more brittle? Lunar empathy
and solar habit each have their pull by which
the tides of self are governed. It

is harder and harder to leave the stiff forest of *I, I, I*
a life cultivates. The trunks of self
thicken, saplings rise, ready to replace

whatever falls. The wafted drift of meadow
in which *I* began has been supplanted. But wind
moves through. Rain slides every leaf. I try

to remind myself, thick and stolid as I feel, much as I'm able
to resist it, to bend. I try to remember how I flew

weightless in an ocean of womb.

       liquescere, liquescere

         and also
      liquefare. To melt.

Amore

liquefare

afternoons in bed, light filtered through the curtain

we manage to drift
beyond singularity

VII. Deliquescence: *The liquid resulting from the process of deliquescing*

This water. This water. This

cloud light liquid shiftless resistance this

rendering of all we might become.

At Sea

On ships, at the restless edge, in kayaks, or the self salt-buoyed: at home at sea.
In car fume supermarket fluster office: here here and again here. At sea.

Paddle the marsh, *Spartina* beneath, wafted. At last
our joy again in each other. We adhere at sea.

Three or four close calls. One with launched life rafts,
distress calls, ship abandoned. I will not be cavalier at sea.

Rendezvous in the gear locker, tryst in dry stores. Unbound
horizon and surge. A pity it's strange to be queer at sea.

The Mae West, the mustang, the gumby suit stuffed with cork, foam,
or the kapok's lofted seeds. Safety's regalia a veneer at sea.

Something about how it holds and is bodiless.
Years when I desired to disappear into sea.

Twenty-seven humpbacks in view, air shaking with birds
over writhed purple bait. Today: nothing in arrears at sea.

Microplastics, emissions, wooded lot gone to another second
home. Hummers on the turnpike. We are a hemisphere at sea.

One week out, distance an ache in my nipples. Five, the domestic
blurs. Letters, sat phone, memory—attempts to draw you near at sea.

Courtesy

Rollers, breakers, chop, rogues, swells, catspaw, combers, riffles:
water conspires so that you will (you will) veer at sea.

Deep breakers sling shattered safety glass up the shore. Actually,
salp chains unfettered & unfathomable beyond their atmosphere at sea.

How to characterize the light this fall? Warmer than ever—
mottled persimmon hills, amber dune, opal cashmere sea.

Tern, porpoise, seal, gannet, sunset, trawler, cumulonimbus: I call them all
out, unsure of what will bid attention. I am an auctioneer at sea.

Unmoored, underway beyond signal and news but for
VHF chatter: we still pretend the frontier at sea.

Mayday, mayday, mayday the bright dance circling a pole, the call,
from the French *m'aider* and which is always sincere at sea.

Us on the stern lashing the broken mast. Beautiful,
your profile against storm, you, who I hold dear, at sea.

Safety line, radar, float coat, fire hose. All tools (like ebb, boredom, flood,
eddy, lust, forgiveness, surge & even folly) to use, Sailor, not fear at sea.

To Find Stars in Another Language

You do not have the story
yet, although its shimmer
is familiar. And the way its source
is dampened by the blanket of words
we make for it. Yes, you know
each word, but not all in constellation.

> *There was once . . .*

To see these stars you must allow
the possibility of the epic. Sail two days
toward the white land surrounded
by a vast, cold moat. Birds
with mythic wings will assess you,
askance, with one of their pale
eyes. Be warned. They are not
your familiars. Their needs do not
correspond with yours.

> *Once, there was . . .*

Then you arrive. And the stars, after all,
are not so unlike those that have tented
all your ordinary nights. They, too, are lonely.
They are lonely. They mutter and wrestle
in glistered conversations. You can't know
if they'll ever settle. Still, had you the right
time-lens, all stars would look like this, would
refuse the stories—archer, queen, dog—
that seem timeless.

There once was a boy who longed to become
There once was a girl who longed to become

Look   Squint   Let every distant light
escape from story's snare and be

III.
Getting Out

You must not know too much, or be too precise or scientific about birds and trees and flowers and water-craft; a certain free margin, and even vagueness—perhaps ignorance, credulity—helps your enjoyment of . . . Nature generally. I repeat it—I don't want to know too exactly, or the reasons why.

—WALT WHITMAN, *SPECIMEN DAYS*

On the Magnetism of Certain Spots on Earth, Like Provincetown

Governor Bradford's wife, Dorothy, was drowned in the harbor. . . .
It would seem that the God of the infidels, which they call chance,
had a hand in this mysterious jumble.
　　　　　　　　　—Time and the Town, *Mary Heaton Vorse*

November. But still the wild light bounced
between sand and sky, uncultured. It was pulling her
apart,
　　　　unlacing what held her.

　　　　　　　　Wind did its part.
　　　　Burrowing, pushing
grains of the new world into her seams, chafing there, rubbing
until the cloth couldn't hold.

　　　　　　　　An accident, then, not fate or
God's will, her fall out of air's strange freedoms.
She had begun, you see, even on the rough journey over,
　　　　even in the dark hold of the ship,
to believe in chance.

　　　　　　Chance that this spit
curled them, chance that the sun, just moments ago,
hit the dunes hard and came to her prayer-like,

as if all her other prayers had been just mumblings,
shadows rather than light.

　　　　　　There should be a word
for what I've come to, she thought as waves made her the first to see

that elsewhere, anywhere, was worth casting off from
in order to land here, in order to come to even this rest.

Washashore, or, How I Came Here

From elsewhere. Seeking. In the fall
after your father's death, the season after
we stood on another beach and tried
to decide if you could love me still.

Via Boston, which I found I did not
suit, no mountains to stare at
from the crowded streets, working port
distant from the city waterfront,
history entrenched in every cobblestone.

Because your friends had a place with
sea-must in all cloth, and you
were leaving for a different ocean
and I needed somewhere to wait
that I might love if I could not love you.

Of Seasonality

Black-tailed, mule, and white-tailed—they wax.
New growth pulsed by velvet, tender, and so
summer's a season of backing. Of moving forward
through greened bramble and then backing
to realign, fitting the amended body.

They have time to adjust.
                          They don't wake thrashing,
confused by the weight and shape (later,
confused by its loss).

                          I am away
again. I am bumbling, mis-weighted, strange.

Someone's proven the mind lies, at least in part,
outside the body. How far
until my mind does not rest on you?

The grown antler hardens. The not-bone
becomes not-tender, its soft fur
unnecessary. So:

    Rub.   Rub.
                A tree now gone
                    of bark in one
                raw spot, pale
        and hurt and beautiful in the dark wood. Then

    bellow   posture   clatter

And the valleys echo or moss takes the sound.

Soon they're shed of weight which
even while splendid was burden,
and at last that season's done.

armor,

VACATION WITH WRECKAGE

Down the beach, beyond the river,
where the dawn-men did not rake
the sea wrack into piles and bury it
in small holes along the water line,
the beach was a mess. We didn't walk there

until our all-inclusive week was almost over.
Nice to see driftwood, shells, bones. Less so
needles and shoes. There was a strange
surfeit of underwear bands—not the panties
or boxers themselves, but what snugged them

looping out of sand. And corners of luggage.
One bolt (I think) of cloth. A seat cushion
with airline script and grab straps. It was vacation.
The sea was blue as Tastee Freez. We bought a stone
dug from the island's center. Polished,

it looked like cheap plastic. Raw, it was
kind of boring. We needed this week.
Drinks and paperbacks under umbrellas.
Afternoon fume and buzz of jet skis
when we'd retreat, undress, reemerge to evening.

returning

What was there to bicker over? What stress
to leach? No phone, no job, no dog
getting visibly older. I admire the work
of the rakers, shore smoothed
after storm surge has tossed up what waves held,

the stuff not removed but buried and there
not festering. Transformed. Love, there is no hidden
rancor in this poem. The sea is gorgeous, the sand
clear, the hazards nothing we need to tend
more than this delight.

Correcting the Landscape

Even though the wrecked jeep
belonged to Pat, it felt like stealing to go through
chain link into the scrap yard, jack up
each corner and switch out his new tires
with our bald ones. It was twelve below.
The snow squeaked underfoot

like Styrofoam. We were trying to make it in a place
where everything we thought we needed
—sheetrock, tomatoes, polypro—
had to be shipped in from Outside.

There was a raven calling, watery cluck
echoing the lot. There was us cursing
the lug nuts, then another sound,
out of place, high and keen

and you and I startle like any goddamn bird.

I see your head tilt, ear
to sky, and while Anne is jumping
blood back into her toes and Pat is wrestling
with the left rear, there is within this scene another:
A peregrine calls and we both look up, catch each other doing it,

then laugh. Because it's not likely a falcon here,
February in central Alaska. The call sounds again,
and a few pigeons startle, birds that arrived with
the wires and poles. And that's why we hear it,

set on some timer to cry away
those pushy opportunists
at the foothills of the Chugach,
throats cold in the day's short light.

EXCEPTIONALISM

It's true, we fought
a few hours ago, window
open to the warm spring,
but we got over it, moved on,

swam in the pond and talked
about the smoke of pollen
dusting everything, even
clothes clean on the line.

And then later,
when voices rose from
the shared drive, she high
and crying, he another self
than when in passing
he waves from his truck,

it was plainly something
with such a deep wrong
it should just go ahead
and break. We were reading

in evening light,
the dog asleep nearby,
her joints released
from pain. A clock ticked.
You rubbed your eyebrow.

The choked sound of
wronged and wronged.
Even earlier, when I
was grating and then pathetic,
when you were chuffing bluster,
that couldn't have been
what was overheard.

INVOCATION

Swagger, clang your spurs
through me. Swing
saloon doors open & push on in.

I'll pour you another, I'll lay down
what needs to be dealt on the green felt.

The back shelf bottles
are dusty, grimed at the lip but sip
and what's in them burns hot

as ever. I'll reckon you. I'll reckon
we've not yet wrecked it, not yet.

Reckon the oasis, too, appears as mirage
so why not chase it. Water's somewhere
under the hot, dry sand.

SEX ON THE AMAZON

Most of the monkeys we see don't have prehensile tails
and pink dolphins seem too creepy for seduction despite
the stories. We're watching howlers swing down

from the canopy. When I first heard them, I was in the water.
I thought they were a storm through rigging but there was
no rigging, no wind, just those males roaring claim

and dolphins beneath my treading legs. I felt
the water they moved but only saw them at a distance.
Back in the skiff, it's all about howlers. Their noise, their

coiling tails. I tell Carlos I've seen orcas in Alaska loll and unfurl
their pink, hidden trunks then twine them in air. Gray whales, too.
Jorge, the paramedic, doesn't understand English, but gets *penis*,

and laughs. We go on. "Most birds don't have a penis"—I make
my hands into tubes, bump ends for the cloacal kiss—"except
ducks." Jorge nods, twirls a corkscrew above his lap,

"por el agua." We laugh in the back of the skiff. I am
the only woman on the crew, the only American.
When I first came aboard, after my name, I was asked

by each man if I had children. "Do you have children?
Do you have children? Do you have children?" Pity,
puzzlement at "No." Only Manuel, who is not the youngest,

is not a father. New to this river, to them, I don't say much.
After a *varzea* walk with Juan, passengers talk about
miraculous plants. One cures bronchitis, they tell me, one

weans a child, and the sap of one can turn a man gay.
I nod, look out past our churned wake toward jungle . . .

> *O tree fronded, twined, scurried and surely fluttered*
> *by morphos deep blue as crepuscular sky yet shining,*
> *surely smooth-trunked and buttressed to allow flamboyant*
> *sway, why have I not seen you? Where do you flourish?*

Five weeks together on this boat, five trips, five groups
for our repeated stories. This time, when Lucho asks
about my husband, I say "she." He doesn't seem

to notice, but they say *she* about each other all the time,
slippage of a romance language. On this side of the Andes,
no one likes Mario Vargas Llosa. In his novel, the women

of Iquitos are hot, loose. Now, they get trouble in Lima.
Pablo's daughter comes to visit the ship. "My baby,"
he says. She is sixteen. When a passenger asks about AIDS,

Javier says it's better now. There are programs and condoms,
there are discos in Nauta and Iquitos and no one throws fruit
during the parade, but (but) hairdressers still travel the river . . .

> *Beautiful canoe cutting the bank, bright feathers*
> *boaed up the paddle's shaft, parasols abloom*
> *above groomed heads and fine shears glinting*
> *like quick piraña, who welcomes you when you land?*

Later, Javier tells me about a gay demonstration
on the cathedral steps—"kissing"—the face he makes
is like a mouth of bitter sap. I know what

I sound like here. *He, she.* Five weeks
together on a boat. We make jokes about
the animals, do our jobs. One day, Carlos helps me

ask a boy if I can try his canoe. They hold it steady, hand me
a paddle, then won't let me go. Ridiculous,
my she-husband, my childlessness, this dugout not built

for the likes of me. That tree—I want to tell them
its sap is the most delicious thing I've ever tasted.

INCIPIENT

She buys a maternity shirt. He says
ooh mommy to her chest. She buys
a laptop so she can work from home
when the baby's born. To test the signal
in the bedroom, they stream porn.

Who will she, my sister, become when it—
future resident of a room stocked
with stuffed animals from our childhood
and games from our grandmother's closet—is born?

Across the country, I vow to learn
Spanish, start cooking with turmeric,
write a different kind of book. No one
will help make me new for you, no one
will distract us.

Weather Station

My father assembled it from a kit, ugly
thing with a faux-oak case. He twisted copper
wires, placed cog against wheel, spring
against lever with his greatest precision
and so made from them all a measure
of wind, atmosphere, and heat.

He climbed a ladder to the house's peak and placed there
the three white cups of the anemometer to spin
down, blurred to a dial of speed, the air's exact
rate. My sisters and I would wait for gusts
to jump the needle red, but not our father.

Every morning, he came down the stairs,
leaned over the kitchen table, and tapped twice
on the weather station's second face.
The barometer's thin hand shivered
to a different rest, then he twisted the ribbed knob
to mark the pressure's shift.

My sisters and I were weighted with sleep,
sluggish as fog, our spoons heavy as a thermocline.
Dad tapped the thermometer. He glanced
at the wind direction, put a hand
on one of our heads, thinking

about gears and wheels, about the curve he'd have
if he graphed the week's flux. So near us,
how could he know what storms we dreamed,
what gales we'd do our best to summon?

At the Source of the Ore Our Smelter Processed, Thus Making Commencement Bay a Superfund Site (or) At Least the Tailings of a Glacier Are, if not Beautiful, not Toxic

On the glacier above Kennecott Mine, melt pool
a pure Listerine at my feet. Clouds & shadows. Distance
unhighwayed, unbridged. No matter the nationality,
everyone on the trail speaks gear: crampon, ripstop.
The red mine buildings are charming, an attraction
giving scale, held by policy in "arrested decay."
Toward the ablating glacier's foot, the ice is tired, grey.

It was not pretty in Tacoma.
Sure, there were nice spots, parks
and a few of the beaches. Some historic `
structures like the jail were quaint.
But, really, we were pulp
mill, dockyards, smelter.

The gift shop, a replica of the store
where miners paid their bosses
for what they needed, displays empty crates
of Washington apples. Warm, tart sun
sent north when ships came up for copper ore.

We fished, swam, ate clams that sucked
the water of the bay into their soft bodies.
No harm to report. The smelter's gone,
the stack that was our horizon mark
for the sun's swing, imploded.
Guys in hazmat suits cleaned the site
for years. Horsetails frond the tailings.

Above treeline, the contact zone is clear:
a line where two rocks meet—limestone,
greenstone—and minerals precipitate. The miners
slept there, bunkrooms frosted by breath,
shaft left cold so they'd work harder. Porphyry's
jagged ridge is stunning, but they wouldn't have seen it
from so close. I bet most of them

hated it here, where it still
is beautiful. I bet they
couldn't wait to get out either.

Eagles Every Day

Local kids put on robes and masks we'd walked past in the museum. Materials (mountain goat hair, buttons, grizzly claws, eagle down) and context (for potlatch, to welcome back the salmon, for the dance of peace).

Elders sang while the kids, in a range of attitude and attention found everywhere, danced. Wolf moved like the back-row guys in eighth grade math class: slumped, habituated. One boy took Raven and *was* the bird— quick stop-start tilt of eye and beak; awkward, menaced hop; a sense of bright mind turned for a while toward you, making you strange.

He must have been thirteen. I could see the shimmer of basketball shorts, baggy and long, at the hem of his robe. And the back of his head under the mask: hair gelled to another sheen.

This at the end of a week among the bays and islands of the Inside Passage. Drip of cedar in rain. Killer whales mid-channel. Swaths of hill bright green where the timber had been sold and taken. Gill net buoy lines. Eagles every day.

∾

I grew up on Tok-A-Lou Avenue, below Mana Wana and Ton-A-Wanda. Above the Puyallup's outflow. On clear days, a mountain that has not yet been returned to its name pinned the horizon.

There was a totem pole on the lawn of my junior high that none of us ever really looked at until Todd and Wade cut it down one night with a hand saw and left it toppled in the grass.

Everywhere, there were stylized logos with Salmon or Thunderbird, tow trucks rendered in form line design. Every year, we bought illegal fireworks from the reservation stands.

There was head-shaking about the casinos and the fishing, talk we'd lose our house to reclamation. I drew pages and pages of black and red shapes copied from a book: ovoid, clean and full of stories I didn't bother to learn.

∾

We sat in the cedar room with a dirt floor and regulation fire doors. We watched and listened. The all-aboard time was 3 pm. That boy's Raven—

We applauded then ate what they gave us: soapberries whipped to froth with sugar and handed out in paper cups stuck with carved, wooden spoons, now ours.

The berries were sweet, then bitter.

We filed out, saying *thank you, thank you.* Sincere. Someone, probably the purser, handed an envelope to the woman by the door. The kids milled out back in street clothes. We walked down to the boat.

PROTECTION ✓

When a friend said *shooting range*, I
pictured hay bales in a field, something
a half-step from Robin Hood. This

was a concrete bunker, ceiling low and pocked
by bullets. When you pressed a button by
your ear, a paper target zipped out and back

on a wire. I liked the protective glasses
and the earmuffs we were given to wear, dull snug
of their hard red shell. And the wall of ammo

was pretty—tidy and logical as the card catalogues
I rifled as a girl. The man who rented us the .22
for six bucks was nice. No swagger or sneer.

Maybe I'd have felt differently if the gun itself
had been more graceful or old-fashioned. But the thing
on the counter was mean and practical.

There was another girl at the range who didn't
touch the guns, who stood against
the folding table behind the stalls

as her boyfriend tried the .45, the snub-nose,
and something else. Just to not be like her,
I wanted to fire at least a couple times,

but I couldn't. I watched small casings
bounce against my friend's left temple as she shot
into dark rings. Next to us, three guys

were working on a target made to look
like some fucker coming at you in an alley.
Dulled, I could hear the shots, the jinkle

as someone shuffled stance. A loud fan
tried to take the smell away. I stood. Blank. The good girl
I thought I'd gotten rid of was taking over, standing

and smiling when expected to smile, mask
tough as Kevlar, body underneath
hot, sour, uncomfortable, safe.

Relative Proximity

We are on Anne's guest bed watching Master Chef.
I am visiting. It's late. My sisters do this every Tuesday.

During a dramatic pause
Anne shifts and looks down at her belly.

I watch as Kate reaches without asking
and feels the baby move beneath her hand.

It Was Daylight

That it was daylight, that we saw the coyote
low under roadside brush, that
it just kept walking and did not

                            turn away.
That there wasn't much traffic and we
could turn the truck around. That we had
the camera and the battery wasn't about to die.

It lay down with a band of sun across one eye
lighting it tawny and deep. Its ears
were taller than I'd expected, fur deep
inside them. When I opened the door and stepped out
it didn't move.

                The next day, you'll call
your sister, even though we're on vacation,
our first in years. I'll go outside and listen
to the cactus wren start and start its rusty engine.
You'll learn your mother's dead.

That it let me step close and the shutter didn't flinch it.

I stared. Silence, a thick band, wove
from you to me to this coyote just beyond
barbed wire. We attended

                       one another.
And whatever lay behind that close watch
was unimportant. Another car
went by. A raven called down the road.

We had nowhere to go. Even though

the next day would be rushed flight. Even though
when I look closely at the photo later I'll see
matted hair and blood above the clear eye. Even though
the stories will have to be changed, then, we felt lucky.

RELATIONAL

I see them now where I didn't—
in airports, mostly, on the dark
chairs before gates, walking

corridors loud with feet and wheels
clacking. Or just outside baggage claim, where
the smokers stand, arms propped up

so the hand with the cigarette
is like a screen, the smoke like a screen.
Grief-crumpled, blotchy, raw. I remember.

I told the ticketing agent. I told the girl
who sold me gum and *Vanity Fair*. I told the TSA guard
because I knew we were distracted and odd

at the scan belt. I lied
to the airline rep, said *my mother* when
explaining, angling for discount. I told

myself and told myself as we
made our way back east:
your mother is dead.

Considering Interference

The pilot announces delay as the left wing
tips to circle and the windows blank in cloud.
I cinch my belt. The woman next to me
reaches into her bag, flips on her phone to check the time.

Calculation: age of phone – airplane mode + bad weather =
uncertainty, uncertainty and *all electronic devices*...

I think of the girls on trial in Salem, faces gray
and flat as low fog, their accused selves
buttoned into dowdy, pious garb. The climate
that held them. The muddle of linkages:

I am the girls, captive; I am the Goody deciding
if what she sees is enough to decry; I am the weather,
uncaring. I am pilot, noose, jet, judge, bemused
and untrue instrument, nervous woman

whose English is just bad enough to make
the drone of announcements worthless.

I am the gap of understanding, the moment it widens,
the endless, shadowed fall of it, the figure mute on the edge,
maybe aware of future regret, maybe just curious to see if it's real.

Getting Out

How in love with myself I was
on the iced-over river, Alaska Range
sprawled miles around, skeered trails
of snowmachines across the low hills,
spruce and spruce and a few hours
of thin blue sky: the day.

Laced into three-pins, sweating
in the perfect ten above, skijor
harness snug on my hips, at last
I was in this February
air silent of most birds, not
in Anchorage's Tacoma-ness, its
five-lanes and conveniences, but

on skis, in the mountains, an old dog
pulling me toward a cabin of logs,
its weather door a thorning of nails,
point out, to deter bears.

Do you know this moment? When
you expand at last from the clench
of the daily, find yourself bodily glad,
at last discovering pride (or whatever word
we don't have for such pure chest-bursting) not
something to be stuffed into a pocket,
but vast and permissible.

some helpful, some because the naturalist in me can't help but help herself to a teaching moment

I.

"We All Want to See a Mammal:" Avens is a nickname for *Dryas integrifolia,* mountain avens, a sweet low plant in the rose family. Linnaeus refers to Carolus Linnaeus, a Swedish naturalist and the founder of binomial nomenclature (ie: *Homo sapiens*).

"The Truro Bear" owes its title to Mary Oliver's poem and book of the same name. And to the bear itself.

"Right Whale: Death as Spectacle:" The right whale in the poem was a female named Staccato. North Atlantic right whales are one of the most endangered large whales in the world, with less than 500 in existence as of 2015. Every individual is critical to the survival of all, particularly females. They are called right whales because in the whaling days they were considered the "right whale" to hunt—they have huge baleen (up to 15 feet long) and, when killed, they float, which made retrieving both baleen and blubber much easier. Luckily Staccato's daughters and granddaughters are doing well and are still seen around Cape Cod.

"In the Inner Harbor:" Northern gannets are a spectacular sea bird, white-bodied with black wingtips and subtle yellow on their napes, the largest species of sea bird in the North Atlantic. Related to pelicans and blue-footed boobies, many winter in the waters off Cape Cod, and their plunges when hunting are spectacular.

"Historic Numbers of Right Whales Skim Feeding off Cape Cod:" In the spring of 2011, scientists and locals alike were stunned by the numbers of right whales in Cape Cod Bay and visible from the shore. Right whales annually come into Cape Cod Bay to take advantage of the later winter/early spring plankton bloom. Although they are enormous, their diet consists almost entirely of a small type of planktonic creature called a copepod—something even smaller than krill. Endangered now, they once were terrifying hazards. Historic texts describe the bays of New England being thick enough with whales that captains were afraid for the safety of their ships.

"Misapprehensions of Nature:" In 2008, a video of "Christian the Lion" went viral on YouTube. The italicized lines are a direct quote from John Rendall, who bought the lion with Ace Berg in 1969 at a London department store.

"On the Habits of Swallows:" There is no blue pigment in bird feathers. The color is generated by light interacting with a feather's structural properties.

"The Problem of Syllogism:" There are a number of species of ray in the *mobulidae* family, most iconically the manta ray, *Manta birostris,* which can reach 6.7 meters from wingtip to wingtip and has a near-black dorsal surface and a white ventral side. Manta rays feed mostly on plankton, and most species have no dangerous spine on their tail. In the Gulf of California, mobulas, as they are commonly called, are often seen swimming in schools, sometimes making spectacular leaps out of the water. The species *Mobula tarapacana, thurstoni, munkiana,* and *japanica* all can be found there.

"Obligations to the Unprecedented:" See notes above for "Historic Numbers of Right Whales Skim Feeding off Cape Cod" and "Right Whale: Death as Spectacle."

"A Further Explication of Irony:" Shearwaters are a sea bird akin to albatrosses. A few species fly the North Atlantic, but none other than the Manx (we now know) nest on the East Coast of the United States. Generally, sea birds prefer to nest on isolated, inaccessible cliffs or islands where mammalian predators are less likely to get their vulnerable chicks.

"Distance Education:" Pushki is another word for cow parsnip (*Heracleum lanatum, H. sphondylium*) a plant native to northern temperate regions and prolific in Alaska.

"Cultural Exchange:" The Ucayali River and the Marañon River come together just south of Iquitos, Peru. There, they become the Amazon.

II.

The poems of this section were written in response to work by visual artists. "Travel of the Light," "Deliquese" and "To Find Stars in Another Language" to lyric videos by Demet Taşpınar and "At Sea" to a sculpture by Janice Redman.

"Travel of the Light:" In Greenland, Inuit would carve wooden maps that they could hold in their mittens while traveling by kayak. "In laboratory dark" refers to experiments done on migratory birds to see if, without the sun's cues, they might know at what time of year (and day) and in what direction to fly for migration. Scott Weidensaul's *Living on the Wind* has some wonderful accounts of these experiments.

"Deliquesce:" Velum is a term for a type of veil-like cloud. Although diving bells did exist before the 18th century, Secretary of the Royal Society of England Dr. Edmund Halley's was the first practical design. It was made of wood sheathed in lead, stood nearly nine feet tall, and had a glass lens at its top. In it, people could stay 60 feet under water for an hour and a half at a time. Diving bells were a huge help in harbor and bridge engineering. "Phosphor" refers to the light emitted by small planktonic organisms. Commonly called bioluminescence, the chemical light is sparked by movement.

III.

"Correcting the Landscape" owes its title to a novel by Marjorie Kowalski Cole. "Outside," capital *o*, is the term Alaskans use for the 48 contiguous states.

"Sex on the Amazon:" We think of monkeys as swinging from their tails, but only a few species on the Amazon River have the capability to grasp in this manner. The penises of large whales (humpback, gray, orca, bowhead, etc.) are indeed able to maneuver like an elephant's prehensile trunk. The bird anatomy, too, is accurate. Not many birds have a penis, although ducks, which mate in water and thus face potential sperm escapage, do.

"At the Source. . . : " Commencement Bay, Washington was a superfund site. According to the Environmental Protection Agency when their website was checked in the spring of 2014, the "EPA placed the site on the National Priorities List in 1983 due to widespread contamination of the water, sediments and upland areas. The Asarco smelter shut down in 1985, but a century of stack emission fallout from smelting operations had contaminated the soils in the town of Ruston and a northern portion of the City of Tacoma with high levels of arsenic and lead. Smelter slag has also been used by residents in various applications.... As of September 30, 2011, all work funded under the Recovery Act has been completed."

"Considering Interference:" In 2015, we are allowed to use our electronic devices like phones and tablets on airplanes at any altitude, but there was a time when certain equipment was forbidden. We understood that it might interfere with the plane's navigation . . . or something.

"Getting Out:" Skijoring is a winter sport in which a person wears a harness on their hips, and that is connected to a dog, wearing another harness, that can then pull them as the person travels on skis.

AN IDIOSYNCRATIC INDEX

ACKNOWLEDGEMENTS

The following poems have appeared in the publications below, sometimes in different forms or with different titles. I am grateful to them.

JOURNALS

Alaska Quarterly Review, "Cultural Exchange," "Deliquesce: A Meditation in Seven Parts," "Incipient," "In the Inner Harbor," "The Truro Bear"

Adrienne, "August Song," "Considering Interference," "The Problem of Syllogism"

Catamaran Literary Reader, "Ritual"

Connotation Press, "A Further Definition of Irony," "An Apology of Sorts," "At the Source of the Ore Our Smelter Processed, Thus Making Commencement Bay a Superfund Site (or) At Least the Tailings of a Glacier Are, if not Beautiful, not Toxic"

Drunken Boat, "Travel of the Light"

Green Mountains Review, "Of Seasonality," "Right Whale: Death as Spectacle," "Sex on the Amazon"

Knockout, "On the Magnetism of Certain Spots on Earth, Like Provincetown"

LBJ: Literary Bird Journal, "On the Habits of Swallows"

Mid-American Review, "The Problem of Syllogism"

New Madrid, "Deer Hunter"

Orion Magazine, "Correcting the Landscape," "Historic Numbers of Right Whales Skim Feeding off Cape Cod"

The New Yorker, "We All Want to See a Mammal"

The Rumpus, "To Find Stars in Another Language"

South Dakota Review, "Vacation with Wreckage," *"Valkyrie"*

Southern Humanities Review, "It Was Daylight"

Superstition Review, "Getting Out," "Misapprehensions of Nature"

ANTHOLOGIES ETC.

This Assignment is So Gay: LGBTQ Poets on the Art of Teaching, "Distance Education"

Fire on her Tongue: An eBook Anthology of Contemporary Women's Poetry, "Of Seasonality," "Misapprehensions of Nature"

Oil + Water, "In the Inner Harbor"

Cold Flashes: Literary Snapshots of Alaska, "Eagles Every Day"

"A Further Explication of Irony" was chosen as the winning poem in the Outermost Community Radio poetry contest.

Poetry Daily, "Incipient"

"Right Whale: Death as Spectacle" and "Historic Numbers of Right Whales Skim Feeding off Cape Cod" were part of a video poem, "Triangulation," that was published on the *Orion Magazine* blog and first screened at "The Whale: An Exploration" at England's National Maritime Museum.

A WALLACE STEGNER FELLOWSHIP enriched the poems of this book and allowed time for their accrual, as did time at the Wrangell Mountains Center and as Poet-in-Residence at Brandeis University. I owe much to those who gave their eye to the poems of this book: Lynn Brown, Christine Byl, Gabriel Fried, Eloise Klein Healy, Sean Hill, Nancy Pearson, Janice Redman, Eva Saulitis, Alexandra Teague and Sarah Van Sanden—thank you. Special gratitude to Demet Taşpınar for the spark of collaboration and the inspiration of a new medium. To my family, chosen and born to: you shape the world that makes it all possible. And Lisa: of course, yet it should never go without saying.